homemade traps
for new world Brians

Evan Willner

BlazeVOX [books]

Buffalo, New York

Praise

These are poems for our new millennium. Evan Willner explores the state, or rather the states, we are in, with fifty poems of remarkable linguistic power. These little "traps" or contraptions of 145 syllables each, take up big issues of our time—the challenge of seeing the self from the angle of the cell; the mechanization of bodies and minds; the violence that accompanies and defeats our procreative urge—and turns them into units of poetic energy. Enjambments, apostrophes, interrogatives pull us in. Words squeeze, ooze, protrude and collide like the mind-body entities, those brains and brain-emissions they describe. The poems wreak havoc on everyday language and associations in order to regenerate them. And if they shock us and amuse us by turns, they always please.

Bonnie Costello, author of *Shifting Ground: Reinventing Landscape in Modern American Poetry* and *Marianne Moore: Imaginary Possessions*.

o   o   o   o   o

Evan Willner reinvisions fifty states as fifty poems that each have the flinty, hard logic and formal density of stone slabs—stele or gravestones—or of teeth. And yet, the language within these poems is palpable and mysterious and alive, the connection between words and things skew in all sorts of right ways that end up making everything seem to be wriggling and formicating on the same level of consciousness: next time you look at nature, don't be surprised if it gives you a come-hither look back. A must read for all Brians.

Brian Evenson, author of *The Open Curtain* and *The Wavering Knife: Stories*.

o   o   o   o   o

Strange things are going on in the dark woods, and Evan Willner has noted them all down – tree trunks, sticks, bones, rocks, jerky turning neighbors, cereal ding dongs and diapers and odd flying things – noted them down in grammatically elegant sentences that marry complex literary processes with the muddy matter of our world and turn them into – bingo! – poetry.

John Tranter, author of *Urban Myths: 210 Poems: New and Selected* and *The Floor of Heaven* and editor of *Jacket* magazine.

o   o   o   o   o

Relentless and pessimistic, Evan Willner's poems track the blurry line between metaphor and metastasis, exploring the dark underside of creativity with intellectual rigor and dark humor. Part phenomenology and part phrenology – these poems constantly "rak[e] [their] hands" along the world's surfaces to find its "packed dumb families" – <u>homemade traps for new world Brians</u> explores the ethical dilemmas inherent in the act of creation. The drama of these poems exists at an almost cellular level – each homunculus a new rejection of the synthesis of subject and object, each poem straining against its formal limitations. Willner's work is difficult, metamorphic, offering itself as an answer to the philosophical questions it poses. Why, in the end, do we create life or art? "So, we can,/when birds flap and bubble, believe that it's us they mean."

Spencer Short, author of *tremolo*. (winner of the National Poetry Series award).

o   o   o   o   o

Scary, abrasive, absorbing poems. Like outer planets orbiting what were once sonnets, and with a syntax that at times seems to be a differential science.

Aaron Fogel, author of *The Printer's Error*.

homemade traps for new world Brians by Evan Willner

Printed in the United States of America

Book design by Geoffrey Gatza

Poems have appeared in *6x6* and *Jubilat*

Cover art © The Estate of Francis Bacon

First Edition

ISBN: 1-934289-44-2   ISBN 13: 978-1-934289-44-0
Library of Congress Number: 2006940040

BlazeVOX [books]
14 Tremaine Ave
Kenmore, NY 14217
Editor@blazevox.org

publisher of weird little books

BlazeVOX [books]

blazevox.org

2   4   6   8   0   9   7   5   3   1

A   B

traps

homemade traps
for new world Brians

preface: "the slot of hollow suns risen"

"There was, thank God, a great voluptuary born to
the American settlements against the diked
bowels of the niggardly puritanical
tradition.... For this he has remained since buried
in a miscolored legend and left for rotten.
Far from dead, however, but full of a rich re
generative violence, he remains, when his true
history will be reported, for" those of us
home grown in his seed spread body valley, bloated
like William C. Williams with the thick billions of
Daniel Boones that haunt our cells, canceratic gene
junk, differentiated, proliferating.

first state: "immediately the urge was on him once more"

The first finch rafted in god blessed and bacterial
or it was broadcast here by weather. Termites were
at home here readying the trees, dissolving their
ringed memories years in a day to hollow owl
holes sphinctered tight to keep out the rot, and the finch
knew what to do: seeds here were seeds, the same bunched mud
toads suckled roots, which means, delivered from the folds
of a predator's mind, it could adapt twigs and
earth (the smallest gesture is a nation of states)
to form a nest, and wait. When others come, they'll re
produce, populate the branches, thicken sky and
feather across the new world their finch memory.

2

second state

When chemistry generates mental worms in the fields
of hollow boned birds' brains, scrubbing them with a raw
sperm spontaneous cloud of craving in the flea
activated dawn, and they can feel their stomachs
surfacing in hunger, then they turn to search for
external worms, while the field worms wriggle like field
worms wriggle, unprovably underground. What choice
do you think they have, made weak for weaker meat, on
the feather edge of self-control? They have just their
scratching mechanism and the mechanisms
for beaking and for hoping for rain to produce
the biological worms that make up birds' minds.

third state

If a man rubbed across and smeared his body's limits
and sprayed thick plugs of come into nature's blanks and
blind spaces, it was only to fill in the day
light with himself so the birds would see it his way,
the trees bob agreeably, to seed field ruts with
the recognizing woodcock wink of his genes so
the clouds would bulge with folding fetus shapes, puddles
and bark would touch like skin he could roll himself up
in until everywhere he turned he'd see himself
in the supplication of nature's faces. But
now when he looks, if he looks, his living babies
only peer back, wild in each stone, and won't come out.

fourth state

Skyscrapers look like unkillable memorials,
the settlers thought, and literal, so they shaped
lincoln log beams with their finchy tools, synchronized
grid and name, and wove cities into sunlight with
divine proportion; in each heirloom loft thick with
thoughts of former tenants they signed their thready names
and came on each other, breeding infinitely
photographable faces that press out from the
towers, faces lined like their much-photographed sky
clocks' faces, until it's a megalopolis
of blued neurons softening under the soft sun,
babbling names, senile, beaming, perpetual.

fifth state

Jerked forward by intimate chemical exchanges,
each walking one of us parts the gluteus sun
light with fine outfolding facial muscles like we're
the visible man. We breathe plastic bags and shop
front glass and ripple; moment wobbles into soft
moment like the wind muscles tree leaves so they pulse
thready green to lit white to flame to green season
in a blink. Asphalt gives with walking time while we
work ourselves through offices and alleys until
you feel like you could peel back hot concrete city
slabs and touch a human blooming musculature
and the pulse we compress into each brick and stone.

sixth state

You were always the one who wanted to make earth face
you, to suffocate in mud folds while you squeeze, fist
and wrestle them into a body, so you took
us in the woods and wallowed in it, spreading and
laughing in your bed mouth, making soup and begging
us in tightening clay skin that cracked and stripped so
we could hear it hissing the words for you, making
us shuffle and humid for you while you wanted
so bad a baby. You were the one who taught us
that something's always trying to bleed out from an
open mouth into the struggling twinheaded day,
semiformed, and that it can be stoppered with earth.

seventh state

Just like a mother voids herself of children and then
greedies up their inches, ages, vitamin in
take accomplishments, so the pork left out all night
is packed with pocket fresh babies their cuckoo mom
deposited, grubby chicks gaping their pleaders
and feeders, asphyxiating tinily in
pork cells or rescuing themselves by drilling air
shafts and mining veins, growing into their fibrous
egg by feeding on it like a mother does when
she suckles at her children's soft facts, their clinging
fat and growing sleep thick heads like milk to hold them
immortal in her organs of recollection.

eighth state

And windows aren't metaphorical like cut glass
hands or hands with lines in them, and the rooms behind
them obviously aren't trees that Daniel Boone
red leaves hung onto, they say, out of family
duty, dry veined and chafed, and then flew off of like
they'd jumped through a window flailing like game buck shot
in rich folks' paintings down like leaves to puddles to
shiver their reflections, obliterating the
gape and the obvious and horizontal sky,
what are you fucking looking at? Windows aren't
public either, so quit peeping in them for some
wishful Boone face to father your rippling face.

ninth state

Then there's the issue of the maypole bodies that pull
us throat tight through our daily turns, turning in day
for day, strung up standing by pulleys and branches
grounded in bone and contracted by hard pulses
and turning through the rotten and slow open mouth
neighborhoods we know we know that squat wood hard in
mud too old to name. Tied by fascia to our back
yard trees and husbands and groceries and watching
our jerky turning neighbors, we've got to take care:
our muscle leashes could tangle, bringing us up
short or bumping us together to produce new
bodies jerked in other tight and turning circles.

tenth state

After the Renaissance buffet is arranged, seasoned
with particle light, justified and shot, and the
photographer goes home, then, in the shutdown dark,
the pert and posed melons, cheese, pork slowly begin
to sag across sagging hours, unpreserved by
curatorial care (how do they keep portraits'
paint limbs, hair, and skin from sloughing and pooling), and
they loosen and spread under forces thrilled to sculpt
chiaroscuric rucks into each apple, slack jawed
in the appreciation, dawning like a skin
of mold, that time is hard and presses faces in
to expressions of age and an ounce of slow juice.

eleventh state

Though their playing at leaping from what look to us like
low ledges, their copulation of muscle and
muscle against fast air, even their six year old
mouths caught static pink and the facts at play when girls
hit the ground can all be described or captured limb
for limb in snapshots, no photograph can show you
the ledges these games rehearse or the waking lengths
they will fall. In this hard square they're yard browned living
muscle, photostop secured, yours; don't ask what else
the toothy air sustained almost earth struck girls are
leaping from, holding hands: they can only laugh and
know that, in due time, they'll do what they have to do.

twelfth state

The wall looked like a wall and bore when he looked its brick
layers, levels, sand, and other significant
technologies. It felt like clocked and mortar crusts,
fat wet cut, molars leveled and faced, sandblasted
lunches, wives; there were other walls maybe, a broke
city's worth, veining the wall, fixed in place and brick
present for him, with children schooled and heated in
digging hours and shift breaks buried there for him – all
the wall's extending relatives were there. He touched
then raked his hand along its brick hard at the tight
dusting shrug of it, the packed dumb families: he
met a wall and everything was in it but him.

thirteenth state

When you undulate all over yourself, processes
surface and press against your skin as if your wrist
and rib bones and your greedy spine were birthing through
your last cheese cloth resistances (puncturing the
bladders that hold the meat and breath economies
separate and immaculately safe from summer's
particulate filth), unsocketing themselves from
your knit and schedules to spread careless with me in
the grass where the sun can tingle every length and
pore of them, and so can I. Sometimes I'm sure each
of your organs and every marrowed recess that
throbs pulls out of you to lie so I can see it.

fourteenth state: *tapping*

If it helps, say you remember tonguing all over
some trees, rooting before psychoanalysis
or prophylaxis, and that cold skin soft amber
arms were bathing in sap. Say that a drill sprayed bird
ecstasy over you, then a maple's infant
mouth inhaled for you and let its glossy ooze. Then
the hand. Maybe a nest was abandoned and you
climbed branches and broke and sucked egg sap until that
orphan taste pours from each egg you've eaten since, from
your blue veined collecting hand, the cracked howling birds
and all your self-serving memories, and dries in
to a skin smoothing over your mind's current folds.

fifteenth state

In prehistory oral nerves were enveloped like
a nervy finger's enveloped by shivering
pudding by the dreaming pudding of an infant's
gums: once upon a time, they floated in baby's
pulp sea mouth, tongued and rockabyed safe with early
warning systems sensitive to a mere needle
vibration of the impending catastrophe –
and then the child learned to bite. The world became
a smeary silk cut so the nerves retreated in
to chitinous shells. Now, in the modern mouth of
sensible morphemes, the animalcule tucked in
each tooth still mumbles with the throb of exposure.

sixteenth state

Pour us into city bodies someone you've got to
rope us tight to stop us from eating and growing
fuller across landscape and richer, assuming
literal numbers whole or muscling them back
with our sweat bright righteous girth blocking what can't be
bodied out or consumed, becoming the country
because why not always and burying in our
inclusive and pooling truth the grain states' ropey
folks, fat gagging lungs. Truss our fear of starving down
please to third world hard life sizes, disappearing
or disincorporating; tell us maybe, if
we're wedged into margins, we can be kept crowd safe.

seventeenth state

When you, your face invaginated and your finger
joint brain articulated over night wet months
of ontogenesis, slip from my blown body
and grow away into your own man, the muscles
that held you in, loosened but accustomed to you,
will hold your shape like a chick mouth gaping pink and
jerking on its neck for any mother who'll feed
her scrap into it, cooing your long gone cuckoo
coos into the forest's slack folds. There's a world of
wombs like mine, distended memorials to slip
aways like you, self sufficient children born free
to lick and ripple their own puddle reflections.

eighteenth state

Then there's the one about the west tending contraction
that pressed a bolus of human matter, skin miles
thick in parts flaking and clouding up to black out
daylight like a hemorrhage of carrier pigeons,
clotting acres, across the plain. In the blown o
pen desert the sea was impossible and bones
stretched rangy and far. Parts are missing here, but there
were gorgeous patriotic mountains more purple
than ten sublimes and trees grown obscenely red and
thick with honey milk for the sucklers who came to
trade with no one, tree fed and valley hot, breeding
termlessly until the ground withered beneath them.

nineteenth state

In the great give and take plains statesmen like us pack chuck
into casings and exhale God's own breaths, swimming
with the spittle, credit and calculus of our
tender concern, into their holes, inspiring them
to cheer and vote; we let them fumble with our law
until we can sew together a more real
istic constituency. In time, our castoff
golems will accumulate, constipate rivers,
gripping cubic tons of drinkwater, a dike of
plush thick pressed flesh, disjected chests, a tumble of
arms groping for loose hasbeen teeth, breathless sick for
wanting, who can't seem to pull themselves together.

twentieth state

This photograph of a man who is about to be
or is currently being bayoneted is
our business, as war correspondents: see how we
captured him realistically in this thin sac
hot square moment so he appears rich with breath and
pressing, like ocean presses the swimmer's two-pound
lungs, against the flat surface of things? That's what makes
it seem like we knew him or like we've seen the hand
pressing its rifle through space until it becomes
invisible before. That's called technique: making
the curt act seem collaborative, as if they'd
wait, posed, for just the right light and then kill for us.

twenty-first state

Believe that finches collect, shout, and fan each other
with our human news – who's on top, in; who's the next
biggest thing. Who's finished – or acrobat, or sing;
believe these moist bone assemblages cradling
their millimeter lungs can love so we can coo
them up to bed like palpitating peachfuzzed girls,
because when we see finches, we want to lie down
in them or just plop them into our mouths to feel
them tumble around us in oxygen bright blood
and become lodged in our brains' gathers. This is why
we have anthropomorphism: so we can, when
birds flap and bubble, believe that it's us they mean.

twenty-second state: *post-mortem on the poet's father's mother*

She made herself some cancer to augment her organs,
teat her veins to its undifferentiated
face, infiltrate connective tissue and thrill her
fucked body with stubborn life. Later, we saw growths
protruding from bronze shoes, stock shares, constellated
jewelry, New Jersey, more: everything she left us
bulges with the mass of her, and all the silver
has this taste against our teeth. This is gramma's in
carnation (Lord, may we see the hilarity
of your face) in each inheritable hold in
the occupied world. This is the infestation
of her love, which feeds on our attention and grows.

twenty-third state

Now you're dead and your furniture is dusted with skin
and talk and livid with roots folding finger fold
on fold, reaching until there's a mass of veiny
articulations at work and warm in the wall
and in the chairs. We can't touch anything without
it spouting gene rich serum over us and we
can't keep ourselves from letting it back into the
struggle of days: we cough up tiny cancerous
bodies that meet, tangle above us, and settle
like a spray of ticks on us who only want to
miss you. You're content to keep sucking yourself out
of us and spitting yourself back into our mouths.

twenty-fourth state

When spring loaded cars bud from far countries and come crowd
your face, pouring tourist babble hysterical
in coats thick over you so you can't breathe without
inhaling their spores and underground garages
disgorge traffic exhaling its superflux math
hot ash to pave over every city pore and
nothing can be done to stop the human bodies'
viral discharge in the subway and they're stuffing
themselves all into your spaces, between legs and
under toenails, impregnating you with their blow
fly sentence and its punctuation – remember:
you're my father and my mother and you can't die.

twenty-fifth state

The pilgrims stood in clouds at the far coast, having rubbed
themselves across every field and alien leaf,
o and buffalo, every object a sunset
pulverizes, slapping the trail to puff it off
their clothes in dust pillars, and engineered themselves
homes on the last bluffs cantilevered out over
sea air so deep whipped with atomized slip rock and
surf froth that it seems solid. Not that they didn't
know better but each one could lean out and breathe, in
the stillness of true religion, the airborne motes
of some once and future pacific land bridge one
thousand miles long that can be crossed but not crossed back.

preface: the workshop of potential literature

Because our capricious given organs tend to leak,
real plastic implants are in development. "One
may compare our efforts – mutatis mutandis –
to that of the laboratory synthesis of
matter.… The remarkable success of present
biochemical synthesis allows room for
hope, but fails to indicate convincingly that
we will be able to fabricate life in the
future." Sure, our technicians concede smilingly,
hands body deep, "the elaboration of
artificial structures would seem infinitely
less complicated than the creation of life."

twenty-sixth state: "there can be no concession"

An infant leviathan preprogrammed and under
whelmed toad, chafed by conditions, will fuss itself in
to mud and tunnel down past root teats through sinew
and clay to the tender marrow states warm beneath
a continent some god had littered with worm arms
flailing their pliant tissue and bone, ur bodies
unable to conceive of elbows or the pull
and lock devices of the puritan toad that
burrows beneath them, bending space to incubate
some two legged posttoad race it dreams of as it
bodies on toward a first deepest torpor, almost
but not quite finding a place to wake from.

twenty-seventh state

A Brian may be delivered, chubby and sulking,
from the vein soaked field that feeds it, by a finch and
laid in the delighted sun heart basket of its
gastrointestinal tract. Swaddled first in in
human acids made to peel away a Brian's
butter to access its secret embarrassment
of meat and sublimate it into the abstract
stuff of flight, and then fisted through the intestine,
fingered dry by slow miles of cilia, taking
it, what's a Brian made for, it'll be crapped back
into daylight and, exposed to the suckling sun,
fold itself into any motherly mud hole.

twenty-eighth state

The first time a homeless face exhales itself over
you, it will atomize, seep into lung sacs, and
black them with offspring, more flawfaced poor that shelter
in your welfare folds, breeding across safekeeping's
gaping lip more faces, mucous masses of them
flowering thick in your throat and working on you
to cough them back into the infected world. Then
do us the favor of covering your mouth and
keeping their needy viral billionfold census
to yourself. Sure, you lack the funds to feed them all,
but the rest of us are as ill-equipped as you
to bear the responsibility of bodies.

twenty-ninth state

Even after its loam filling has dried, the doll's skin,
marinated in hours of salivating light
ly digestive attention, left out in weather,
reposed, held open and photographed, garbage dog
loved, moved by automatic kicks and wind, preserves
when held to light the glistening look of a thousand
tricking knit wool eyes. So who could pick up and take
home this dribbling crease, a drag around pay for
play dolly you'd keep off dry clean only couches?
Who'd rub its bare stitches that stutter on the edge
of purposeless public tears with each spit of rain?
And who could have created this inconvenience?

thirtieth state

The pipsqueakiest of mechanisms you hobbied
together hum like you hum, and the homemade plots
that unfolded awkwardly in your image still
echo around your junky backyard, listing and
peeping for you, increasing in frequency and
self interference while inside you execute
your latest project. What if one sees you in a
puddle and tries to fold itself back into your
placid and loving looking face as indifferent
to its siblings' alarms and rope rescue attempts
as you are, although they spring and catch for it and
for you, their genesis and their face in water?

thirty-first state

If all tagalong creation insists on being
what it's not, rocks dying to skip downhill and spread
out gravel at our feet, hurricane trees to fly
close, everyone caught in your photos to smile and
perform some realistic gesture, the sky to
empty itself all over your face, human feet
to grasp, throat meat so much to be the ticklish air
that threads its variable muscle clutch, and you
to be filled choke full with words ground together in
tectonic poems – and everything just aspires
to a moan – then this crunching must really be the
gravel begging beneath our feet. And if not, not.

thirty-second state

This leech drinks mineral rich life from the hearty chest
she discovered, drilling the veins of a body
builder, a land mass depilated against re
cognition, a man reborn, an American
beloved when he bares and bulges his clean public
borders. He supports, unaware, this leech that taps
his soft walled plumbing and licks at the midnight wet
back blood being hushed and hurried through veins to float
in arterial tenements and feed the pure
buttermilk bulk of his wealth from basement kitchens.
These nobodies are that penny taste of blood our
man washes and washes in his heirloom heart's pipes:

thirty-third state

this is how the infant bundle, hemoglobin thin,
is nourished. It struggles blind and indefinite
under the bodybuilder's shirt, a skin pouch de
pending leech feebly from his chest, willing itself
his stock of mortal oil and making itself the
daughter of his memory. In time, the breathing,
milking leech will pocket two drops of blood, peel a
way, and recirculate them in alien swamp
economies. It'll communicate his stored
generations to its children's children – this fresh
pink flimsy angel who can wear flesh away while
adding an ounce of vealish fat to the father.

thirty-forth state

The sheer pet flesh pawing your chest like groupies, homemade
engines designed to pucker and lip nourishment
from your hand, are, to be frank, very small and can
easily be broken: in their struggle against
swaddling gravity they can tumble into cups,
jumble to pieces or else explode in teary
shrapnel, so you collect and reassure their limbs,
let them sulk on your finger, your coo and succor.
But if you slow down for a moment to tongue sweets
up from your memory and sit and suck yourself,
these infant reactors, jealous, will break down, re
asserting the tiny tyranny of their being.

thirty-fifth state

Seeing Brians exhuming themselves from sidewalk cracks
crawling maybe with Brian seeds and Brians that
come pouring like the savage preAmerican
dead pour out of road cuts and ground breakings, our pores
and each incontinent stitch and labiation
scratched or worried into our property, spraying
themselves all over us, loving so hard – needy
fetus wrapped knots of time that jerk and cry so we
can't tell what's wrong with them or make it stop –, shouldn't
somebody cram them back in where they belong and
tight dike the fissures they lick through to be with us
in today's breached and quickly drowning cavity?

thirty-sixth state

Between you and me, given the Brians that feeble
after us, are you my mommy, on their pivots
and mud soft limbs, visibly ticking and leaking
ropes of slow gummy pleas for a jaw, some fresh skin,
just one more bone, a colon, fill my courage sac,
throwing themselves from high bookshelves at us, hiding
in hampers with one do me so I'm done eye, what
well formed and forgiving god, seeing our Brians
pleading under a plastic replaceable night
like atheists to any atheist stone, to
us and each other with moist toy senses, would see
to our deformities? Who will own up to us?

thirty-seventh state

Say to yourself that pigeons silk the buildings sliding
under their wraparound shadow or slip over
your face a blush dark hood. Say you can see inside
their catchable meat their susceptibility
to age, disease, or the reality of a
stone at the end of a thoughtless fast string that brings
birds down, and say that's why they never stop circling
breath thin through daily physiological states,
sick with the sun. Now say to yourself that at night
pigeons outrun their feeble shadow. And if it
helps, awake niched and still, you can say their hollow
problematic shapes haunt you like you haunt yourself.

thirty-eighth state

We stood firm in the face of our Brians, swaying back
sliding fat dolls prone to worship any mud god
or wrong homemade doll, and apportioned them in lists
and prohibitions; we drafted each letter, pinned
back the flay of sacrificial decencies, where
and in what manner they were to be offered, how
to script flesh, what was to be done with surplus blood
and limbs, etc., and how to stand, being
counted, split, and counted again. We held our men
upright by the spine. Now look at them, their muddy
faces collapsed back into one mountain abscess
face too sickeningly pinned open to look at.

thirty-ninth state

When wrecking balls punch mouths into a skyscraper, it
exhales one mississippi two mississippi
a tongue thick accumulation of tenant dust –
years of parchment soft feet, sleep, hair and friable
insulation, every membrane that has settled
over other breathing membranes to become the
packed piled organs of our city – all over the
surrounding skyscrapers' open windows; there are
machines for everything, even ones that can purge
our disease from apartments, a blown century
of communicable bodies, all the talk and
brick remainder that congeals in the city's lungs.

fortieth state

When bodies burn down the street, popping arclights pouring
hushing bullet glass down on them and tearing free
from their limbs and skidding skin across TV screens
eyelidlike and they're pitching like teeth through windows
and walls spilling out each others' smeary secrets
on film and filling themselves hard with what can be
grabbed from a shelf and stuck into a cavity,
and, reinforced with stereos cereal ding
dongs and diapers, crash through the city and spread fat
sizzling sweat into our homes, then somebody hold
them hushing close, or count them, or shoot them – but do
something so we know there was something to be done.

forty-first state

The internal combustion engines flare euphoric
nostrils, spark, and jerk musculature in spastic
praise of us – soft gods who were moved on the face, did
the vast necessary calculations, and breathed
will into twists of plastic steel, activating
in each one years of pull and pushback electric
pulses. In living gratitude our offspring shout
justificatory bang-bang and puff spreading
and undegrading hosannas to our rundown
flesh, our folding lungs and tar paved cilia: they
are perpetual incense engines of under
standing bathing us in their gracious tailpipe sleep.

forty-second state

Even the skin of your boots ripples with leaf breathy
impulses while you sleep and twitches as if your
feet were slowly filling them with bone, veins, and meat.
If you let them, they'll slip into the dark where
roots will become leg muscles for them and branches
bowels; they'll make themselves a grass skin body an
y senseless chill can set vibrating with the mud,
the hide moon, the entire night ensemble of
breathing leather instruments it's strung up in. And
when frost tightens and snaps the tendon web, you'll wake
and see yourself jigging jag chemical joy in
your boots outside your window under no one's will.

forty-third state

Say there were a few pounds of flesh folded over and
in over thickening months in an underground
uterine facility until they were or
gans, feeding tubes, knowhow, connective gristle and
convenient limbs; and say together they made a
body, scalpel and plier curious, which thought
about picking its wife's lock, scooping the private
alien disease that had gotten wrapped in her
dreaming intestines as it grew, and inserting
itself like toasty solace into her organ
free cavity. Of course it would find her stuffed with
stubborn jungle fascia and necessary parts

forty-forth state

and as uninhabitable as all the other
quick indivisible creatures that smear across
the landscape when it merely touches them with its
gentlest spreaders, animals that flap throatily
away from a curious feller, make a break
for it, dig, spine, go dead or spray when it only
asks if one maybe could pocket oneself into
their hospitality, just another organ
snuggled among their inwoven organs. No? Of
course not. Silly question. Left alone, it can still
ball up in its own homemade nesting doll states tight
like skin that loves the muscle sliding under it

forty-fifth state

(Understand that when we came with our milk sweat and hard
jawed American anatomy, we were some
bodies. We claimed this semiworld of the semi
human as far as maps can map, dividing each
forest, field, field bird, and nude field native, come on
in it's fine (and they did), into states. We made us
a golem nation – a real garden of living
tubes nourishing liver and lungs. So how could we
have known our cartography would carve out surplus
limb hugging Brians that gape their fill me fish and
fowl poverty across our state lines, catching as
catch can our unapologetic semimilk?),

forty-sixth state

pore rich and penetrable: it had invented these
taut squares to hang in paper plies together all
tits and vowels for it and be habitable
turkey carved into states; it had made its own junk
able machines, careful to withhold only the
unnecessary organs, sure they'd do poppa
proud, sleepy guys that it could cut, slot into and
occupy – but in each incision's plastic lips
white cell Brians appeared, frothing and choking its
access, chewing crying wherever it stuck a
finger. They seep from its curiosity and
if unchecked would pour from everything it touches,

forty-seventh state: "decently ambitious but lacking the raw talent"

so now our intestine tightly folded cerebral
hero sits facing the body suits that it had
stitched together, come on in it's fine, from frank strips
of prose. It wants you to know it didn't think it
would be like this: its experiments on a cut
and touched world are inconclusive, the bodies it
measured and cavitied swing blue with time, brown with
crusting time, and they swarm with spontaneous life –
slappably bashful worm faces, surfacing and
gone, crowd the meat it had painstakingly unpacked.
More and more in the public bodies it makes, un
justifiable Brians seem to take its place.

forty-eighth state

When our gardenheaded Brians discover they'd been
named, like we were named, like mud stick dolls someone
sewed together, packed with ticking and clots of wire
that work them through incontinent fields, folded like
cortex to remind us of us, and made to look
realistic like us with turning eyes and dark
thumby eye fat are named, then they'll run their fingers
down over their faces like someone fingering
a face just to make sure does, just like we do, and
express from the pouches they find swelling there their
own sucky clutch of Brians so they can put names
like fingers into their little garden organs.

forty-ninth state

One more permutation of genetic letters will
produce the last living Brian, the final word
in Brians, thank apocalyptic God. Fine, but
what if it's viral and learns to communicate
itself through blood and raw mouth work from creature to
immunodeficient creature struggling to spell
itself or inks into insistently fertile
animal gaps until every finch and finch flea's
pulmonary moist spaces brew Brian letters
and each terrestrial shape, each secret future
gnat so much as imagined in this infected
world cell, to the nth generation, is Brians?

fiftieth state

When our cities have settled into their concrete old
man clay foundations, having been given hard in
to the continent until it healed over them,
and thick generations of us have filled the sky
scrapers' numbered columns, and even our offsprung
colonies are stuffed to bursting, then surely some
throwaway one of us will touch down on new earth
finchy and all business, or else Americans
made redundant will slip their Mayflowers up soft
core beaches somewhere else. So you can rest easy:
as long as our crawling bodies still fuck on dig
black and smother this skin, we'll have our somewhere else.

Made in the USA
Las Vegas, NV
01 February 2023

66569507R00037